SPECIAL ILLUMINATION:
The Sufi use of Humour

by

IDRIES SHAH

The Octagon Press
London

SBN: 90086057 X

*Printed and bound in Great Britain by
Tonbridge Printers Ltd., Tonbridge, Kent.*

If you want special illumination, look upon the human face:

See clearly within laughter the Essence of Ultimate Truth.

Jalaluddin Rumi

SPECIAL ILLUMINATION:
THE SUFI USE OF HUMOUR

Gar tajalli-i-Khas Khahi, surat-i-insan bebin:

Dhat-i-Haqqra ashkara andaruni khandan bebin.

"If you want special illumination, look upon the human face:

See clearly within laughter the Essence of Ultimate Truth".

This important statement by Jalaluddin Rumi, one of the greatest of all Sufi masters, directly contradicts such numerous sourfaced religionists as, in all persuasions, find that humour disturbs the indoctrination which is all that they usually have to offer.

It is not even too much to say that the distinction between the deteriorated 'Sufi' cults and the real message is found in the answer to whether the supposed mystic has a sense of humour and works with humour.

Although this position is, through the proliferation of bigots, hardly credible to their numerous victims throughout today's world, it was not always so. Plato, if you remember, said:

"Serious things cannot be understood without

humorous things
Nor opposites without opposites."

Looking even at relatively superficial aspects of the sixty jokes which follow will certainly bear this out.

The ease with which a humourless bully — wearing the appropriate expression and wielding the necessary terminology — can convince unreflective people that levity is next to blasphemy is one of the causes of this situation. This is very far from saying that such a horror can actually be right.

I recently came across a 'justification' for humourlessness in religion from a distinguished prelate who expects his audience to be so obtuse that they will believe that Christianity should be approached with misery merely because there is "no surviving record of Jesus ever having laughed." This aberration — known as proof by ridiculous assumptions — was not challenged by his audience, it is true. But the proverbial child in the crowd might well have wondered whether he could not therefore do anything which Jesus was reported to have done, including cursing . . .

Luckily, in more contemporary and therefore better documented systems, there is ample information:

"I have never seen anyone who smiled more than the Messenger of Allah", said Abdullah son of Harith, one of the Prophet's Companions. The Prophet Mohammed was famous for his sense of humour.*

I do not know what religious persuasion Robert G. Ingersoll adhered to. But he said in 1884: "No man with any sense of humour ever founded a religion."† How ever did he come to this conclusion? One suspects it is for the same reason as the prelate. His method of reasoning, if this is the case, is indeed "proof by ridiculous assumptions".

*Cf. my *Caravan of Dreams*, London, 1968, p.23.
†Prose-poems and Selection, 1889.

Let us look at some of the spiritual and psychological traditions of humour, and note how they work. If we do so, I think we will find that the real reason why certain humourless individuals try to prevent the investigation of humour in religion by claiming that it is not there or is antipathetic to it, is that they themselves are insecure characters who dare not enter into the area of laughter . . .

Spiritual studies, people are saying, are far too specialized to leave to the professionals. Where these professionals are those who have turned such studies into morbid charades, this is undoubtedly true.

Traditionally it has been noted by genuine mystics that the professionals, those who have no enlightenment but plenty of obsession, can be easily discovered because they lack a sense of humour. Humour, here, be it noted, is not to be assumed in those who merely giggle a lot, or those who understand only the banana-skin variety: indeed, these two forms of behaviour are the types most often found in pseudo-mystics.

As a shock-applier and tension-releaser and an indicator of false situations, humour, certainly to the Sufi in traditional usage, is one of the most effective instruments and diagnostic aids.

Since I have published quite a lot on Mulla Nasrudin, it is widely assumed that I confine Sufi humour-teaching to researches in this figure. We shall see that adequate joke usages can be found much more widely than the Nasrudin-figure: but the recent history of the Mulla's esoteric role is in itself interesting from the humour point of view.

Some orientalists, not having heard of humour as a teaching-aid (although Nasrudin is mentioned as a master of secret wisdom in an English translation of some of his tales going back over 100 years) have naturally accused me of trying to 'create' the Mulla as a teaching figure. I had, of course, "made it all up". Not very long afterwards, a traveller who had resided in Pakistan and carried on Sufi studies through Nasrudin tales, published an article on this in an inter-religious journal. When the original critics were taken to task by a journalist for their jumping to conclusions, their spokesman said: "Of course there is no truth in it. The article must have been written and planted by Idries Shah!".

Now, of course, the pendulum has swung back, and there are people everywhere trying to prove that their own jokes really contain wisdom, and I receive batches of them almost every week, and several books are being busily written by people who will cash in on this trend. They don't know much about the subject, but certain scholars will have to work out how to handle this fact. In so doing, they will be following almost the same path as the Nasrudin joke when he was found stealing vegetables.

Wondering

"Now", said the gardener, "why are you in this walled garden?" "I was blown over the wall by a high wind". "And how did those carrots get uprooted?" "They were scuffed out in my fall." "And what is there in that sack?" "Hold on, I was just wondering that as you came along!". At the moment they are just wondering . . . . . .

Quite one of the most fascinating discoveries in the literary exposition of humour must be what might be called the 'conjuring trick effect'. Everyone knows the feeling of bafflement and intense curiosity to know how a conjuring trick has been performed. What is its secret? Then it is explained to you. The pressure and tension of mystery are suddenly gone: something has been taken away, leaving a gap. This is the chief reason why magicians tend to refuse to 'give away their secrets'.

When writing about or explaining in lectures how jokes work, what they are used for, or how they have been able to exercise startlingly effective insight-impacts and are highly prized in seemingly austere spiritual circles, this effect is strongly evidenced in the reactions of critics and audiences. Reviewers write that "these are no jokes at all"; or that "you are making too much of too little"; or feel that "the explanations are unworthy, superficial". And yet, if one resists the temptation to explain, the jokes can be used with effects which do not produce such opposition, but tend to be appreciated and applauded. Now why is this? First of all, some of the observers are obviously hostile from the start — looking for something to criticize. But these need not detain us, as they would, as the saying goes, 'demand wetter water' if such a thing were possible. They are suffering from what I have called 'the need to oppose'.

The sense of disappointment which comes from finding that the explanation is not as dramatic as the expectation led the observer to suppose causes this let-down and the consequent sneers.

The most frequent form which the manifestation of the disappointment takes is the bluster: "how can a *joke* be spiritual?"; "that doesn't sound very profound to me . . ." What is really happening is that the baffled, not to say frustrated, commentator is in the same sort of position as the boy with the fly. It will be recalled that there was once a boy who caught a fly and dismembered it. He was left with a head, a body, wings and legs: but he couldn't find the fly itself anywhere. What he had failed to observe was that when assembled and operating, the parts which he had in his hand *were the fly*. They operated as a fly, and could not be regarded as not a fly. The fly flew. And the flying of the fly, notwithstanding the bafflement of the boy, was the exercise of one at least of its functions. Similarly, of course, the operation of the joke, before being dissected, is undeniable. It is not the fault of the fly if the boy cannot understand how and why it flies, or how and why its parts don't look like the complete fly. Hence, of course, when we are dealing with an observer working at this level of superficiality, we are under no obligation to conceal what really amounts to his stupidity.

We once carried out a specific illustrative experiment to demonstrate this limitation of the scoffer. Four philistines, generally however regarded as people of some intellectual penetration, had decried the possibility of the psychological, let alone the spiritual, action of humour, claiming that they could "do just as well themselves." When challenged to do so, however, two refused to demonstrate their understanding of jokes. The other two, who sportingly accepted, were unable to provide any structure analysis at all of the stories. A perhaps uncharitable spectator remarked at this point that here was an illustration of the incapacity of people accustomed to power without responsibility: you don't have to be able to do something if you can put up a plausible enough case that it is not worth doing. But these humbugs could be taken as an example of the possibility that, as Professor Robert Ornstein once said: "People who think that they have big brains more often only have big mouths".

You will find that people who have been conditioned by ideology and trained to peddle dogmas often conceal this under a cloak of reasonableness, or have deceived themselves so much that they have a kind of two-tier life. They may appear to be eminently reasonable, but conceal beneath this a lack of flexibility and a series of blinkered attitudes which they are practised at keeping hidden. They cause people to adopt their beliefs because of this camouflage; they are also insusceptible to deeper feelings. The way to flush them out is to test whether they can endure humour or not.

This is one of the reasons why Sufis use humour . . .

Jokes are structures, and in their Sufic usage they may

fulfil many different functions. Just as we may get the humour nutrient out of a joke, we can also get several dimensions out of it on various occasions: there is no standard meaning of a joke. Different people will see different contents in it; and pointing out some of its possible usages will not, if we are used to this method, rob it of its efficacy. The same person, again, may see different sides to the same joke according to his varying states of understanding or even mood. The joke, like the non-humorous teaching-story, thus presents us with a choice instrument of illustration and action. How a person reacts to a joke will also tell us, and possibly him or her, what his blocks and assumptions have been, and can help dissolve them, to everyone's advantage.

The Flame

There is a story, perhaps apocryphal, said to be told in Japan. An American tourist is being shown around a shrine; he and his guide come to a light burning on a kind of altar. "That flame" quavers the aged Oriental custodian, "has been burning for a *thousand* years . . ." The American leans over and blows it out. "Well, it's stopped now, hasn't it?"

I have heard this tale told in perhaps five different countries. When the tourist is British, the implication is that he scorns the whole thing; when it is a Frenchman, that he feels himself superior; when it is American, that he is insensitive. The last time I mentioned this fact in rather august company, I was taken to task for having so little sense of humour myself that I either wanted to spoil others' enjoyment of a joke by analysing, or trying to wring meanings out of it where none was legitimately to be obtained.

But I see jokes like other people regard, shall we say, oranges: they have both experiential and nutritional content. The fact that a fruit tastes delicious does not mean that it cannot have food value. If I smell an apple and enjoy this, it does not mean that its nutritional value will be ruined if I should eat it. This argument has, it is true, been combated by the suggestion "Ah, but if you smell a rose you enjoy it, but if you try to eat a rose-bush you will be disappointed". Luckily for those who don't agree with this assertion, this can easily be refuted by saying that, while we would probably not find anyone who would eat rose-bushes, we can find quite a number of other people who share the experience of perceiving value as well as enjoyment in jokes.

I myself prefer to note that the character assumed by the American in our story of the flame shows him, if we assume that he is like other Americans whom we meet, to be experimental rather than reflective; more anxious to do something than to score a point by talking alone. It is this general characteristic which makes me think that the intense interest taken in Sufic studies by Americans of all kinds, including supposedly rational, sober and well-established ones, is far more constructive than it is designed to gain something, either, that is, to gain by scoring a point or gain by consuming something. Many people will not agree with this. In answer, I can only invoke that delightful, if somewhat ungrammatical, English phrase: "I speak as I find, and you can't say fairer than that".

People who are unsympathetic to spiritual matters can certainly have a sense of humour; although it is not necessarily completely effective. Sometimes their jokes are more revealing of themselves than of others — but sometimes these jokes can give us a yardstick to measure some of the adventurers whom these anti-religionists take for the real thing.

The Dollar

There is a story that when destiny was being planned, the archetypal representatives of various peoples and schools were offered their choice of gifts.

The Japanese asked to be given the Zen koan, so that people would always be attached to the power of perplexity. The Hindu guru asked for the mantram and the assertion that everything was derived from his philosophy. Then an American-to-be was asked for his choice. Since he was to be one of the last peoples to emerge, most of the more attractive things had been handed out. But he was not long in asking:

"Give me the dollar — then they'll *all* come to me, sooner or later!"

This could certainly account for why the United States is a country where every cult and religion, every theory and system, has sent its representatives — and, on the other hand, it might just account for the presence in the U.S.A. of the mercenary ones from overseas.

The Recipe

There is a story told by Sufis about a man who read that certain dervishes, on the orders of their master, never touched meat and did not smoke. Since this tends to fit in with certain well-established beliefs, especially in the West, this man made his way to the *zawia* (assembly-place) of the illuminated ones, to sit at their feet. They were all over ninety years old.

Sure enough, there they were, not a spot of nicotine or a shred of animal protein among them, and our hero gasped with delight as he sat drinking in the unpolluted air and tasting the bean-curd soup which they provided. He hoped that he would at least live to a hundred.

Suddenly one of them whispered "Here comes the Great Master", and all stood up as the venerable sage came in.

He smiled benignly and went into the house, heading for his quarters. He did not look a day over fifty.

"How old is he, and what does he eat?" asked the enraptured visitor.

"He is one hundred and fifty years old — and I don't suppose any of us will reach that venerable age and station", wheezed one of the ancients, "but, of course, he is allowed twenty cigars and three steaks a day, since he is now beyond being affected by frivolities and temptations!"

Hidebound attitudes towards the religious life, which have crystallized out as a result of certain processes and abstinences being carried out for limited periods and for specific studies being adopted as sacrosanct, have to be broken before progress in higher religious studies can take place. I am quite sure that many of the supposedly anti-clerical jokes found in the East and West have this very same important intent and function. They are not, that is to say, the work of scoffers, but of illuminates.

Nowadays we even have stories told in the East which purport to be re-imports from the interplay of the cultures now happening in the West:

The Background

The first Eastern mystics were seen in America about seventy-five years ago, and there has been plenty of time for a whole undergrowth of tales about their adventures to grow up in their home countries.

One such story concerns a prudent guru who did not want to waste too much time in cultivating people who were without sufficient prestige and collateral. He was introduced, it is said, to an American widow who was reputed to be very wealthy. Having learnt a thing or two about how things are done in the West, he asked an enquiry agency to check her out.

When he opened the report, it said: "She has a million

dollars in the bank but will probably not have it for long, as it is reported that an Oriental phoney is trying to get his hands on it."

One of the characteristics of many truly metaphysical jokes (that is, tales and quips intended to jolt the consciousness) is that they are viable in several different ranges of meaning. As I have noted elsewhere, this is also one of the cultural requirements of a good story. In order to ensure the durability of a teaching-tale, it must be one which will be preserved, through retelling, even by people who have no idea of its inner values . . .

Here is a story which may be taken as an anti-Sufi joke, while it also means that 'aversion-therapy' can only be done successfully by those who know how to do it:

The School

There was once a dervish who went to a certain country to set up a 'school'. As the months passed, he found that there was another mystical master in the vicinity who had convinced people for miles around that mawkish senti-mentality was the same as spirituality. So most of the people who came to sit at the feet of our dervish were influenced by this very same outlook. He realised that he had to get rid of them, so he went away for a pilgrimage, leaving behind a message:

"I have decided that the other dervish is so good, so pure and so holy that I must go, and ask you all, dear disciples, to follow him, for he is so much better a man than I am . . ."

When he came back, he found that the other dervish and all *his* disciples, having heard of this wonderful act of self-sacrifice and honesty, had come to join *him* . . .

Unwitting humour is sometimes as good as anything intended to be funny. Many of the "Land of Fools" jokes are of this kind, and some of them emerge from interaction with people who think that they can think, or feel, or

15

something else, when all that is happening is that they are inwardly pursuing some obsession or clamouring for attention. I quite often get this result when analysing people's reactions to books.

People write to me constantly noting that I say that Sufism is not learnt from books. They don't ask me — never have so far — why I write books on this subject: they only ask how they can learn without books. People who think like that (asking someone who writes books how to learn without them) are unlikely to be able to learn in either manner. I generally put them in touch, if I have the time, with the smaller but still significant number who understand that literature is (a) preparatory; (b) capable of provoking experiences; (c) able to interpret experiences; (d) likely to help people to avoid problems which would prevent them learning — and many more things besides. It is interesting to note that this automatic response, this half-understood reaction, is itself a sign that the books should be more carefully looked at before such a person can do any more.

I must say, though, that the most amusing response of this kind that I have had was from a man who wrote:

"You have written so much about the confusing effects of reading the wrong literature, that which is written by muddled scholars and self-appointed 'masters' that I have decided to stop reading altogether."

Some of the best jokes are unconsciously made.

One can sometimes illustrate a psychological truth of value in religious studies by putting the idea into a profane framework. This is the instrumental or operative version of Sufi teaching, and is the higher-level equivalent of the way in which religious preachers use worldly parallels to illustrate supposedly divine truths — the parable, defined by one schoolboy as: "A heavenly story with no earthly meaning."

16

One such tale concerns the persistent claim that one should not charge for knowledge, even though everyone also knows that people do not value something which they have got for nothing.

One of the major activities of Sufi teachers is to elicit a picture, a profile, of the kind of mind, the pattern of conditioning and assumptions, which make up the intending disciple.

One classical — if usually more concealed — instance is told in this joke:

Belief

The master was at the height of his harangue:

"And if I were to tell you anything of what I really, deeply know, you would not believe me. If I were even to hint at the truths which are understood by those who have attained to Truth, you would scoff; if I were to give you any statement of the amazing realities behind what you imagine to be reality, you would not credit it . . ."

A member of the audience held up his hand: "Surely you cannot expect anyone to believe *that*?"

No Service, no Charge

A man went to a physician, feeling very much out of condition.

"Ah, yes" said the doctor, "you must do this and not do that; you must eat this and drink that . . ." and he droned on for a time.

Presently the patient started to walk out.

"You haven't paid for my advice" said the leech.

"Ah, but I am not taking it!"

It is very true that people don't value things that they get free. Equally, of course, for what it is worth, they won't pay for things if they don't intend to have them. . .

A joke will sometimes help a disciple to see his real

situation: though not always at the very moment when it is told. Anyone who has been any kind of a teacher will know that certain pupils do not want to learn, but blame the teacher inwardly:

Trying harder

A disciple had been attending the discourses of a certain teacher for some years without saying or doing anything.

Finally he called him in for a private talk.

"I have been giving you exercises and teachings for many years now, and I fail to descry any change in you, and I am becoming perturbed" he told him.

"I am glad that you have noticed at last" said the disciple, "for I have personally felt for some months that you are not trying hard enough!"

As I have noted, jokes which are familiar as just ordinary jests can be seen to have psychological levels which can be quite striking when transposed into the spiritual situation.

They have been used for centuries to hold a mirror up to people, so that they can see their own behaviour in a way which is otherwise very difficult indeed.

Many quite unsuitable people try to attach themselves to teachers and teachings. Their unsuitability, more often than not, stems from the fact that they want to do or think exactly what they want to do or think — and they want to have all this approved as a 'mystic way'.

Just as good

One such person — a woman in this case — kept plaguing one teacher, who — for something like twenty years — found it necessary to refuse to allow her to seek 'heaven' through divining cards, enigmatic books, mysterious rituals, perfumes and disembodied voices. He did not allow her to use Oriental names, to spiritualize the physical or to physicalize the spiritual.

Finally, when she had become very subdued, he realized that she was only biding her time and would again start demanding secrets and processes instead of just teaching. He decided on a memorable once-for-all interview and counsel.

"Here at last are your instructions" he said. "You will drink some holy water, fast for three months and repeat this word ninety million times. Then you will walk to Katmandu, measuring your length along the way, never lose your temper, strain every fibre to hear celestial music, and never say a metaphysical word. Then you will stop doing all these things and go back to ordinary life as you know it!"

"O Master!" she breathed, "and I will then be in a state of perfect freedom and release?"

"No, but you'll feel as if you were!"

Many people probably know this as a familiar doctor-and-patient joke: but note its relevance in the discipleship context.

There is much unconscious humour to be met every-where. I recently managed to 'get through' to a circle of people who were posing (or rather their master was) as illuminated:

The Secret

I visited some self-styled Sufis who proved to be nothing other than — in their own eventual description of themselves — pious frauds. They claimed to have a 'secret teacher' who knew everything, but whom one could not meet. This is one of the latest gambits, by the way. When he was run to ground by someone else, the following dialogue took place:

"Are you the Secret Teacher?"

"Yes".

19

"But you don't know anything about Sufi teaching."

"That's right — but that is the Secret".

Those were people who did not know what they were doing. There is a tale about one who did know: it was the observers who did not. . .

One of the most difficult things to teach is that Sufis may teach without the excitement and attention, without any of the externals, that people desire and believe are a part of higher teachings. In the Western world, for instance, there would probably be very little room for a silent Sufi.

Yet there are in fact silent dervishes, as well as the whirling, dancing, howling and jumping ones.

But people are in many ways similar all over the world, and a tale is told of the Silent Dervish who came to settle in a village, where the people did everything they could to make him talk, so that they could get some teachings from him. They were unable to still their desire for stimulation by him, and as a result they were not able to perceive that he was continuously emanating baraka and teachings which they could otherwise have absorbed.

One day, when he decided to move on, he thought that he would give them a hint of his function, because although he was a Silent Dervish, they wouldn't believe it.

Last Straw

People brought him food every day, and he always ate it. One day he had not, and when the people arrived with their offerings, he said: "You can take this away!"

"But why have you never spoken a word before?" they clamoured.

"Well, the food has always been all right up to now!"

It has taken something like 100 years of exposure to energetic missionary work from the East, notably India, for people in the West to realize something that a very large number of people in the East have known for a very long time. This is, of course, the fact that a lot of gurus do not know the simplest facts about human psychology — and even physiology.

The next joke has been repeated for centuries and startlingly well illustrates that contemporary knowledge of gurus by the populace was often greater than that of the gurus about the secular:

What was needed

There were once two mystics talking. The first one said: "I had a disciple once, and in spite of all my efforts I was unable to illuminate him."

"What did you do?" asked the other.

"I made him repeat mantrams, gaze at symbols, dress in special garb, jump up and down, inhale incense, read invocations and stand up in long vigils."

"Didn't he say anything which might give you a clue as to why all this was not giving him higher consciousness?"

"Nothing. He just lay down and died. All he said was irrelevant: 'When am I going to get some *food*?' "

People are always asking me why I have to rely to such an extent upon Middle Eastern knowledge of metaphysics, and why I cannot disinter fragments of the 'Western tradition' which will indicate the existence of a long-standing awareness of the levels of spiritual understanding.

Here, then, is one instance which I take as showing that anyone who tries to graft spiritual practices (we are of course interested in higher perceptions) upon an un-regenerate personality will end up with an aberration. I need not emphasise that there has recently been a period in which thousands, perhaps millions, of people in the West have tried to 'storm the gates of Heaven' by trying just that. This joke gets them into perspective, if we realise that it is *they* who are the cannibals and not the African in the story:

The people who think that they are religious — or, equally, 'on a higher level of perception or mysticism' — have in fact suppressed the real spiritual side, and are living on a social, a shallow, level.

Ritual for its own sake

A missionary who had been captured by cannibals was sitting in a cooking-pot of rapidly heating water when he saw the cannibals with their hands clasped in prayer. He said to the nearest one: "So you are devout Christians?"

"Not only am I a Christian", replied the annoyed cannibal, "but I strongly object to being interrupted while saying grace!"

The carrying on of automatic habits, of intellectual sophistries without a change in the person, or of emotional activities without deep perception acting upon the real self, cannot ever be the same as the experience of the mystic.

If this tale is taken as a parable of trying to make someone rise to a higher state without transforming his lower aspects, it can also serve as a classical instance of the Sufi argument that human beings must clarify their personalities before they can attain certain desired levels. Let us call it the 'incompatibility of coexistent tendencies in the individual'.

I have noticed, during the past fifteen years or so, that the ideas which we have put forth are increasingly being adopted as cultists adjust to the new knowledge. So let me give you a joke which should warn against adopting the cults which have clothed themselves in the Sufi raiment just because it is less tattered than their own:

"Sometimes", a man was saying, "so many things have been borrowed by my neighbour, I feel more at home in his house than in my own. . ."

But the gurus who do this kind of imitating should beware. Something happened to one of them when trying to get some information on Sufi ways, which he least expected. Incidentally, such developments are not uncommon in Sufi history, but I will go straight on to the true story:

The Burden

A man called at the house and asked if he could come in for a few minutes, as he owed me a great debt.

I had the distinct impression that this was someone with no real metaphysical or traditional psychology interests and I was sure that he was, as we sometimes — I am afraid — say, perceptively dead.

I immediately asked him what this debt was.

"Your writings have released me from a great burden."

I told him that I did not believe that he was at all improved by anything he had read . . .

"No, it is what has happened to my daughter."

I said that I did not know his daughter, and that my writings were not designed to release people's daughters from great burdens.

Would he tell me exactly what had happened? I realised it must be something on the mechanical plane, of a sociological nature, not connected with anything deeper, I told him . . .

"Well, that figures" he answered, "you see, my daughter was in the hands of a terrible guru who completely dominated her. He started to read your books and became so infuriated that he died of a heart attack!"

NOW THIS IS A REAL JOKE: IN THE SENSE THAT IT NOT ONLY HAPPENED, BUT IT ILLUSTRATES THE DIFFERENT PLANES OF UNDERSTANDING AND MISUNDERSTANDING, INCLUDING THE FACT THAT WHEN PEOPLE (NOT THIS MAN) IMAGINE THAT THEY ARE 'TALKING SPIRITUALLY' THEY ARE ONLY ON

23

THE SHALLOWER (THOUGH CERTAINLY IM-
PORTANT) LEVEL OF ORDINARY HUMAN
LIFE.

Nowadays, as always, people are anxious to obtain
secrets and gain higher consciousness by short-cut
methods. They hear of exercises and want to use them to
get something done. This is so widespread, especially in
the West, that anyone will try Yoga, people think that they
can gain spiritual insights through meditation alone, and so
on. So this joke, understood as a parable of such people's
foolishness, is not untimely:

Lucky

An oil-drilling millionaire went to a dentist, who said:
"Which tooth do you want me to deal with?"

"Oh", said the tycoon, "drill away anywhere: I feel
lucky today!"

By putting a situation into another context, while
retaining the structure, we can illustrate what is really
happening. This is not so very different from, say, getting a
child to attend to an arithmetical problem by speaking of
apples and onions instead of 'ones, twos and threes'.

It is interesting to observe that this joke will be
extremely valuable in teaching the illogicality and possible
harmful results of adopting random exercises (and most
'mystical' experiments are in fact random experimentation).
The translation into apples and onions from ones, twos and
threes has in such instances really worked. It is almost as
absorbing — though not so heartening — to note that
many people cannot learn from the joke, presumably
having too much capital, as it were, tied up in their
exercises . . .

Another principle which observation supports is that, in
all studies, as in most other aspects of life, people will tend
to seek things which attract them, rather than what will suit

them. Indeed, it can be supposed that there would be no vanity industries if this were not the case. The object of Sufi preparatory study, however, being to illustrate, expose and out-manoeuvre superficial ambition, jokes have come into being to illustrate examples of this tendency in order to prevent it being employed in choosing teaching procedures.

The principle may be enunciated as 'People want what attracts them or will purport to give them what they think they need. Sufi teaching attempts to clarify this and also to provide what they really need.'

This quip is illustrative.

What he wants

A man went into a pharmacy and asked for hair restorer.

"Certainly — a large or a small bottle?"

"Definitely a small one — I don't want very long hair!"

This factor is sometimes known as the 'slightly-deaf' one: the victim only partially registers what he wants or needs.

This is illustrated by the woman whose daughter invited her to her wedding in some far-away country. The mother was delighted to hear that the girl was getting settled at last, and also, as she understood from a long-distance phone call, that it was to be such a suitable match. She sent her blessing and hurried to the spot.

To be married . . .

As soon as she got to the jungle clearing where the preparations for the marriage were warming up, she seemed rather distraught, however. "What's wrong, Mother — you told me you were delighted?"

"I did — but why didn't you speak up: I thought you said a RICH DOCTOR!"

People hear what they want to, imagine what they hope

for. The Sufi saying has it: "God, to the bee, is something which has TWO stings!"

Many of the reasons for people starting on spiritual or advanced psychological studies and then abandoning them are to be found in the single factor of the disparity between their expectations (based usually on conditioning or greed) and reality. They wanted certain experiences but were offered different ones.

It is, of course, difficult to provide people with any version of a truth which they cannot yet perceive, in order to convince them that is worth seeking: hence the vacuum into which all kinds of expectations rush.

Some dervishes, themselves not teachers enough to realise this, have tried to instruct by analogy, only to find that the analogy itself is not suitable. The tale of the dervish who walked on water is employed to warn against this attempt:

Why he did it

Since, by definition you cannot pass on the incommunicable, a certain dervish cast about him for a way to convey, by demonstration, something of the wonders which he had experienced.

"Analogy is the answer" he said to himself, and put his mind to it. . . .

He learnt, after a great deal of trial-and-error, how to walk on water.

Then he called all the local villagers together, headed by the Mayor, and paced slowly across a lake.

"What do you think of that?" he asked them as he arrived at the other side.

"One thing puzzles me", said the Mayor, "why didn't you learn to swim, like everyone else?"

Jokes either stay in the mind or can be recalled to provide usable frameworks for reminding one of this memory

26

difficulty. One Nasrudin tale is used for this and, characteristically economical, also deals with the problem itself: the tale of the shoes.

Teachings often have to be explained or experienced many times before they become established, because of the competition of subjective ideas — the filter through which teachings must go in the ordinary person who cannot give full attention to them.

Shoes

The Mulla was up before the magistrate, accused of stealing a pair of shoes.

"Nasrudin", said the judge, "the records show that you were accused of stealing a pair of shoes five years ago!"

"Yes," said the Mulla, "and *you* just try making a pair of shoes last five years!"

One of the paradoxes I have noticed is that people who do not remember things that would be useful to them are generally those who are in too much of a hurry: their very agitation and impatience slows down their progress in the end. People constantly write to say that they feel that they have so little time, or that they must do this or that urgently. If there ever was a case of 'If that is your question, you will never be able to understand the answer' it is in this situation. But one can give a certain answer, again a joke, which has been observed to produce good results:

Painting

The way in which to answer this while giving an analogy is to mention the man who was asked why he was painting at such a tremendous rate. His answer was:

"There is so little paint left I am terrified that it will be finished before I have got this door covered!"

It has often been said that everyone has higher

perceptions, but that effectively they have none, due to the barrier effect of the 'heedlessness' (the Sufi technical term is *ghaflat*) which prevents understanding of something already, so to speak, known.

One of the major causes of this heedlessness is not to take equal note of all the materials which one is offered. Accustomed to choosing what appeals to them, people do the same with Sufi instructional materials. The result can be summed up like this:

Muscles

There was once a man who took a correspondence course in muscle-building. When he had finished, he wrote to the firm which supplied it, saying, "Gentlemen — I have worked through the lessons. Please send me the muscles."

And people too often mistake one thing for another. Having heard of miracles associated with religion, they believe things are miraculous, when they are not, or try to find the miraculous, rather than the truth. They won't listen to a source of knowledge, even, as the saying goes, when they are sitting up a tree with one. Perhaps the saying comes from this tale:

The Explanation

Three explorers — a priest, a businessman and a Sufi (whose other interests we do not know) were passing through a dangerous jungle.

As the days went by, the number of hostile wild beats who circled around them became larger and larger. Eventually they had to take refuge in a tree.

After a council of war they decided that one of them should go for help, since if they stayed as they were, fear, hunger and fatigue would eventually force them to fall into the jaws of the ravening beasts.

But they could not decide who should go. "Not me," said the Priest, "for I am a man of God, and I should stay to comfort whoever is left behind."

"Not me" said the businessman, "because I am paying all the expenses of the trip."

The Sufi said nothing, but suddenly pushed the priest off his branch. He fell to the ground: and immediately a fierce pack of hyenas picked him up, fought off all the other animals, and placed him reverently on the back of the largest of their number. Then, guarding him carefully, they escorted him towards safety.

"A miracle!" cried the businessman, "and after your cruelty, divine guidance has intervened to save that good man and I am, from this moment on, converted to a good and holy life."

"Steady on" said the Sufi, "for there is, after all, another explanation."

"What other explanation can there possibly be?" shouted the businessman.

"Simply this: that it takes one to know one" said the Sufi "and the smallest always recognise their leader and honour him. . . ."

It is the inability to perceive truth, because of self-deception for which there are distinct remedies, which causes people to accept 'teachings' from 'teachers' which are really no such thing. Pseudo-teachers, too, fall into the same trap, as is so thoroughly known in the East as to have produced this familiar story:

Tasks and illumination

So-called spiritual teachers often do not know what they are doing. But, as they can hardly confide this to everyone, they are relieved when they can discuss the consequent difficulties with one another.

Thus it happened one day that when two pseudo-masters of the mystical path met, one said to the other (after the customary exchange of compliments):

"I have a disciple who constantly asks for tasks and illumination. Have you any idea what I might do with him?"

The other illuminate replied:

"It is interesting that you should say that: I have had a similar case myself. I had him drink a cup of kerosine."

They parted and, after some months, met again.

The first mystic said: "I tried your idea on my disciple. He lit a match to have a cigarette, burst into flames and was completely consumed!"

"That's right" said the other, "the same thing happened to mine. . . ."

I was talking, not long ago, to one of the 'dancing dervishes' who sometimes travel to the West to demonstrate the whirling movement originated by the great mystic Jalaluddin Rumi of Konya. I mentioned to him that Rumi had said that his practices were instituted for the temperament of the people of Asiatic Turkey, not for Europe and America. In accordance with Sufi practice, exercises are devised for specific time and people. Did he not think that it was rather unusual to 'export' such things as this?

He told me that, since people in the West automatically associate music and movement with spiritual things, this was bound to arouse in them feelings which they considered to be spirituality, which was, surely, good enough for them?

The Bottle

It all depends, of course, what you are purporting to be doing; but this puts me in mind of a story about Mulla Nasrudin when, camping for the night, he put a bottle down as a pillow. "Mulla", said a friend, "surely that is going to be too hard?"

"As an ordinary bottle, yes" said Nasrudin, "but I am going to stuff it with straw before I put my head on it."

Humour is often used to help people remember that one is often so literal-minded, or so responsive to conditioned reflexes, that ritualism or slogans take the place of understanding or even action.

This example, making use of the English idiom, illustrates what could happen, on the social level, if such thinking were to become prevalent in ordinary matters. The effect on spiritual matters is held to be analogous:

Escape

A convict had escaped from the prison in a storm, and the Governor was informed. He reacted immediately: "Send out the cats!"

"Surely, sir" said one of the warders, "you mean 'Send out the dogs!' "

"Certainly not. I wouldn't send a dog out on a night like this!"

People often imagine that if they do not get what they have wanted exactly when they want it, they have wasted their time, or that someone else is to blame. They may think, too, that they are to blame when it is all a matter of the right time, right place, right people.

You can keep this in your mind by an analogy, which is not supposed to be regarded as a sacred recital, but is scripted to show you the relative positions of timing and also of how people leave out of calculations things which alter circumstances. This is the story:

A Wager

A man once bought a parrot. When he got it home, he told it: "I am going to teach you to talk". "Don't bother," answered the bird, "I can talk already!" He was so amazed that he took it to a teahouse. "Look, I've got a fantastic talking parrot here!" But the parrot wouldn't talk, even though the man kept insisting that it could. People bet him ten to one that it could not, and he lost the bet. Nothing would induce it to speak.

On the way home, followed by the jeers of his friends, the man cuffed the parrot and said: "You fool—look at the amount of money you lost me!"

"It is you who are the fool," said the parrot. "Take me back to that teahouse tomorrow and you'll get one hundred to one and win!"

'Time, place and people', of course, is the message. Keeping this principle in the mind helps to make it operative. This in turn alerts one to the 'occasions' when progress in higher awareness can really be made.

Once this idea is firmly grasped, and can be recalled, it can be attached with great effect to the next principle, which concerns background. One may be able to perceive something when the attunement of time, place and people is arrived at; but unless one has also developed a sufficient understanding of ability to 'decode' what the 'messages from beyond' mean, this effort is wasted.

We can invoke a tale here to allude to what happens when results are achieved with an unsuitable vessel:

The Meaning

Following more than fifty years of atheism, scientists in Russia began to be curious about what religion might be.

A group of them took a book of holy quotations and decided to have it decoded by an analogical computer.

They opened the book and took the first phrase they saw, typing it out onto the keyboard.

The phrase was "The spirit is willing but the flesh is weak."

They crowded around the print-out as the words began

to appear. As they read the message, their astonishment increased:

"The vodka is ready but the meat is devitalised."

"No wonder religions used to mystify people" they muttered to one another.

Then one of them had an idea. He tapped out the book's title (*Unconsidered Trifles*) onto the decoder. Out came the translation: "Neglected Puddings".

"You see" he shouted, "you have got the wrong book — this is one about the abuses of cookery . . ."

They are still seeking an authentic religious text.

Sufi humour-teaching often concerns itself with the need to have the right information and the right experiences, in the right order. Some people who believe themselves to be sensitive to deeper perceptions, often show themselves not even to have a share of them.

Too much trouble

A man — so goes the ancient Western joke — went into a place which had a sign outside: "Any kind of sandwich served."

"I'll have an elephant sandwich" he said.

"Sorry, Sir," answered the waiter, "but we cannot cut up an elephant for only *one* sandwich."

In the famous Elephant-in-the-Dark story, of course, each person has grasped *some* part of the elephant. We could use this Western tale to emphasise that you cannot taste a scrap of higher consciousness (the elephant) even though you might be able to 'buy' a scrap of something which you might think to be similar — say a cheese sandwich . . .

The foregoing story is a useful test, too, of the existing awareness of students. Setting aside the fusty obsessional who hates such tales, the most usual reaction is that the waiter is being clever, and has outwitted the cocky customer. Those whom we find to be more able than others to direct their attention, however, will often remark that the story also indicates that there is a useless tendency to draw ineffective conclusions from materials presented to one.

Those who cannot see this immediately can usually do so after they have been exposed to this associated tale:

The Meaning

A certain professor was demonstrating, before fellow-members of the learned Academy of his country, a remarkable discovery.

First he took three flies out of a matchbox. Then he commanded them to fly three times around a table. Then, on his command, they jumped five times. Finally they danced a silent tap-dance on a table, their images magnified through a gigantic apparatus devised for the purpose of making such things visible to a large audience.

The onlookers were spellbound. "And now" said the scholar, "I will give you the demonstration. It is the illustration of my discovery."

He took the flies and placed drops of honey on their feet, sticking them to the table. Then he shouted: "Flies — jump!" The flies went on licking at the sticky stuff.

"And that, gentlemen," concluded the Professor, "demonstrates that flies, when their feet are covered with honey, cannot hear!"

Believe it or not, the two preceding stories are unfunny to people who are suffering from one of the characteristics which may link the Professor and the sandwich-bar customer: small-mindedness causing inability to understand. In ordinary life this is usually seen in people trying to get more than they can out of a situation where they eventually lose.

This is excellently portrayed by another Western — an American — joke, about trying to get things on the cheap:

Value

A man had just given a beautiful girl a ring set with a flashing stone, as big as a walnut.

The girl said: "Is this a REAL diamond?"

"Well", said the man, "if it is not, I have been swindled out of three dollars!"

The opinionated nature of the pseudo-teachers who often pass for real ones, especially in the Far East, is a byword. Here is a story currently in use among legitimate gurus there, which never fails to confuse or annoy the (sometimes very celebrated) frauds. It always has to be tested, however, by being recited without any intimation that it is a joke:

Written all over her

A certain rich American lady was visiting an Indian guru who accounted himself as the greatest of all. He had been told in advance that she was thinking of making a very large donation to his work.

When the time came for the guru to appear at his *darshan* — reception-time — he saw this visitor in the crowd which had come to pay respects.

"Yes?" he said to her at once.

"Who is the greatest man in the world?" she asked.

"CORNPONE U," answered the guru with hardly a moment's hesitation.

Afterwards his chief assistant asked him why he had given such a strange answer. "What secret wisdom is in this, O Great Master?"

"Well," said the mahatma, "I of course knew that the greatest man in the world is ME. But when I saw from the inscription on her T-shirt that she respected someone else, I said to myself, "business is business! After all, he's probably dead, so there's no harm in honouring him . . ."

Yet Sufis often answer people in a manner which they do not expect, and such answers do, indeed, cause difficulties. This is generally because the hearers are too full of themselves to profit from what has been said or done. One story helps to fix in the mind the need to observe the occasion and the content, and not to relate everything that happens to one's existing neuroses or preoccupations:

Violence

One day a fox went up to a mouse and said: "I am the king of beasts!"

"Of course you are", said the frightened mouse.

Then he saw a kitten. "Am I not the king of beasts?" he snarled. "Yes, certainly" said the frightened kitten.

He caught a rabbit, and then a hen, and finally a mole. All agreed immediately that he was king of the animals.

Suddenly he ran across a lion, standing in a clearing. The fox ran up to him, crying that he was king of all beasts.

The lion said nothing; but he struck the fox a blow which dazed him and then roared in his ear.

The fox got shakily to his feet and limped away. "Force is no answer to speech, you know," he said. "I have ruffled your feelings — and all you can do is to get violent."

Sufi schools have a glamour which attracts both the quite unsuitable and that part in many people which is not the side which should connect with the teaching. In reality, Sufi study is hard and unpredictable. People must learn what they need to know, not what they may think they want. The external appearance of things, which sometimes has included music and dancing, strange garb and regalia, importance in the community, the air of secrets and achievement, all these may have a place, but they do not constitute Sufi study, any more than the externals of anything are the same as the basis, the root, the reality, the work which goes into producing the effect or the appearances.

Not unnaturally, imitators and people who imagine Sufi things to be the externals alone organise ceremonies and initiations, gatherings and groups, studies and so on, including emotion-arousing so-called 'teachings', even books and recitals, which have this attractive quality. Some people never find out that they have been, in fact, consumers, of externals and vanities, not spiritual people at all.

There is a very old story, couched in religious terms, which attempts to convey in a graphic manner a structure to keep in mind when aiming for real things, not to be diverted by one's attraction for the stimuli which are in reality superficial.

Preview

It is about a man who died and was met by an angel who said to him: "During your life you were always of a mind to believe that things over here could not really be as bad as you thought. Would you like to see Heaven and Hell and choose your own destination, just as you have always chosen in your earthy life?"

Of course he agreed, and the angel opened a door, marked 'Hell'. Inside there were revellers and people dancing and drumming. A constant debauch seemed to be going on, men and women cavorting, demons and sprites prancing about. It all seemed very active and interesting. Then the angel threw open the door marked 'Heaven'. Inside it were rows of smiling people, sitting and lying around, in a state of aseptic bliss. But it all seemed rather cold.

"I'll take the first one," said the man, because he did not want to spend all eternity doing nothing.

They went back to the first door and the angel opened it. He found himself pitchforked into a cavern full of flames and grime, soot and fumes, with demons lashing the inmates and a constant roar of thunder. Painfully and breathlessly he struggled to his feet and stopped a passing devil. "I was taken on a tour and opted for Hell. But it wasn't anything like this!"

The demon grinned: "Ah, but you were only visiting at the time. That was simply for the tourists!"

They say, of course, 'give a dog a bad name and hang it . . .' And there is no doubt that until recently in most human societies there were powerful conventions which ruled all the representatives of traditional psychologies, unacceptable unless they were sickly sweet (when they could be called 'good and saintly') or rough and objectionable (when they could be ignored as beyond the pale). It is these factors which have shaped the outward behaviour of many esoteric teachers, both true ones and false.

They have been, in a word, an oppressed minority, forced to accept the external roles and labels imposed upon them by a society which had its own objectives, none of which, to be fair to it, included the objective of the understanding of man (and woman) by mystical methods.

This meant that Sufi — and other — insights could not be fed into the mainstream of human concerns except in disguise. A Sufi book, to be accepted, had to be superb literature or to contain remarkable poetry. Scientific and other contributions had to be made anonymously. Sufis had to organise secretly: and were then accused of being secretive.

Nowadays things are very different; but, as with all manner of other areas of human life, the news has not penetrated very far, so that you will still find people persecuting those who say and do things which the persecutors feel threaten them.

To give you an analogy, there is the story of the Sufi who was captured by fanatics, and this tale is told by all kinds of other oppressed minorities:

Tricky

The Sultan decided to have the Sufi matched against some wild lions in an arena, to entertain and warn the multitude. Many thousands turned up. The Sufi went into the arena, caught the lions by the ears and threw them out of the ring. The crowd went wild. Then the Sultan ordered him to be bound hand and foot and elephants to be stampeded over him. By split-second timing he managed to roll away from the elephants' feet. The crowd roared.

Now the Sultan had a pit dug, the Sufi buried in it up to the neck, and ordered three powerful and skilled swordsmen to cut off his head. As they struck, he moved his head this way and that to avoid the swipes, so that they started to tire. But by that time the crowd was on its feet, yelling, "Stand still and fight like a man, you tricky mystic . . ."

Just as the problem of the ordinary person is to understand that appearances are not necessarily reality, so it is the problem of the teacher to help to bring this realisation to such people as might profit from it:

What he was there for

A man with a rosary around his neck, wearing a hooded cloak and sandals, carrying a begging-bowl and with a long white beard, was surrounded by a crowd in a certain town. They clamoured for his blessings and he led them to the top of a hill where he sat in silence for several hours.

Finally someone approached timidly and asked him to address them.

"I know that you have all been waiting for the words of

the Great Teacher so-and-so" he said, "and I hope that his visit to this town, which is now over, has conferred the customary blessings upon it . . . But MY own job is now finished, as he will have passed through the streets in our absence . . ."

"Then WHO ARE YOU?" shouted a frenzied worshipper.

"Me? Oh, I'm the decoy . . ."

It can be a matter of sheer survival for the Sufis that they manage to convey the reality of unperceived experience, like the story of the scholar who had to prove to illiterates that he was really reading a book, which we will come to in a moment.

The Sufis always claim that their experiences are such that they can only be perceived by people who are able to understand what they mean, and that this, in itself, is due to a special attunement. This all sounds very much like double-talk to many people who are hostile or fear that they are only dealing with a pretence. But, since at the lowest level it is possible to see that there just *could* be an analogy, Sufis sometimes explain things in the following way to scholars:

Proof

A scholar, in his own life, can have experiences in dealing with people outside his field or on a different level which are not so different in degree and perspective from those which a Sufi encounters in his own.

One day a scholar ran into a gang of bandits who threatened to kill him. "I think you are a spy or a police agent" the chief said.

"No I am not — I'm only a poor scholar" said the unfortunate captive.

"How can you prove it?"

"I can read from a book".

"That's no good to us: we're all illiterates. How do we

know you will really be reading, and not just making it all up?"

So they killed him. "I didn't become head of this band of outlaws just by believing everything people told me, you know," said the chief. And his wisdom was, of course, unanimously applauded by his men.

The attributing of one's own characteristics to others, so common among — for instance — generous and stingy people alike, needs both illustrating and fixing in vivid tales. The brevity of the tale enables one to shock someone out of this habit-pattern. The need to point out the syndrome is there because Sufi understanding cannot come to people who are too extensively self-deceived. To imagine, therefore, the other person's motivation is what is actually one's own is self-deception.

Sufis have built the necessary 'shock' factor into some of these jokes by indicating within them the possible fallacy of certain facile assumptions. In the following joke, the persistent belief that a learner should get everything free is amusingly turned against his miserliness:

No Charge

A greedy and opinionated man, who at the same time had a little superficial potentiality for learning, asked a Sufi teacher to take him on as a disciple. He had first prudently ascertained that the Sufi had never asked anyone for money in exchange for knowledge.

"I will accept you, on one condition", said the Sufi.

"Name it" said the confident miser.

"That you first of all give me six months' income."

"But you should never charge money for wisdom!"

"The charge is not for the wisdom. It is to compensate our school for the bad reputation we'll get for being frauds, if we admit people like you!"

Humourous puzzles, known to most school-children,

are in ordinary circles used only for recreation. The Sufi employment of them is to provide illustrations of ways in which the mind works. Certain Sufi exercises, for instance, have to take place to provide stepping-stones for further development of understanding.

Crossing the river

A Sufi's disciple wanted to know why he not only had to repent, but also subsequently to repent his repentance. Well, he was told, repentance is something someone can do to some extent; repenting it is because you have to get away from self-centredness. But why not do it in one move? This is where the story comes in:

It is like the case of the man with the three things to take across a river in a boat, when he can only take one at a time, and some of them are more vulnerable than others.

He had a cat, a mouse and some cheese. The solution is to take the mouse over first, and leave it on the other side while he fetches the cat. Then he takes the mouse back, to carry the cheese over. Last of all he returns for the mouse.

This kind of explanation offers something midway between an elucidation and an allegory: an equivalence.

Sometimes, of course, the explanation is followed by questions which, although not humorous, elicit further clarification of the story. For instance:—

Q: "But couldn't he put the cheese or the mouse in a box, so that they couldn't be eaten?"

A: "If he had a box, we wouldn't have a story. If disciples could learn in the way they think they can learn without teachers giving them structures — there would be no need for a master!"

The supposed elusiveness of Sufi concepts and experience is found, on experience, to be nothing of the kind. Sufi experience is difficult to register in the mind only for those who are too accustomed to cruder impacts: rather as the sound of a watch ticking will not be audible to someone deafened by a church bell or even listening for a factory hooter.

It is interesting that things which move people powerfully in an emotional sense are often taken by them to be spiritual things. Primitive or ignorant people, of course, actually worship (until they learn better) as miracles or divine, natural things like thunder or manufactured things like guns. Although historians, anthropologists and psychologists know this and have reported it widely, this primitive reaction lingers, especially in 'developed' countries. A sensitive or low-key experience is not sought, prized or understood where there is a cruder one. I would call this diagnostic of whether a person knows about higher perceptions: can he work with subtle ones, does he see the crudity of violent ones?

There is an analogy in the tale of the two small boys who were discussing sweetmeats.

Feeling is knowing

"I wonder" said the first, "why it is that we always buy the jawbreaking candy, when that soft stuff is so much sweeter?"

"I buy it because I like to KNOW that I'm eating something!"

The Sufic objective is entirely different. Someone may be learning in Sufism, although unaware of it. Better still, he may be learning by subtle means which are equivalent to the taste of the candy, not to its toughness. It is almost classical in the Sufi context, in fact, that it is only after the cruder stimuli are no longer craved that the real learning can take place.

You might say that there are two 'selectivities'. People are alerted to things which are familiar to them or to things which activate one or more of their emotionally-linked perceptions. These habits leave a great deal of unused human capacity in the more sensitive range, with which the Sufi works. In order to do this, however, Sufis always have to learn about overall attention as well as concentrated attention.

Selective reading, following only the things which one decides are interesting or central to Sufi — or any other kind of — knowledge, can produce ludicrous results, if it does anything at all. This has been called 'making a comb without the teeth'. I rather like one story intended to help the learner register the need to attend to all aspects of a teaching story, or of instructions given by an authentic teacher, or even procedures handed down from antiquity:

The honeymoon

A man was seen, dressed in exotic finery, whooping it up in the streets of a city. Someone asked him why he was doing it. "Why not?" he asked, "I *am* on my honeymoon!"

"But where's your bride?"

"Oh, she's been here once before, so she stayed at home!"

It has been said that a 'tactful teacher is no teacher at all.' The reputation which some Sufis have traditionally had for being ill-tempered is undoubtedly due to their being primarily concerned with getting their objectives reached, rather than caring what socially sensitive but spiritually dead people might think of them.

If we apply the Sufi test to the majority of the people generally accepted as spritual teachers or mystical masters, there is no doubt that the majority will insist that the Sufis are not spiritual at all (because they equate spirituality with gentleness at all times); while the Sufis will tend to ignore the others as being engaged in social, tribal, community — but not comprehensively spiritual — affairs.

Tactful guru

I was talking to a certain world-famous spiritual teacher who was always surrounded by disciples and followers. I realised from what he said that he did not approve of the things people did; in fact he complained quite a lot about them.

"They want to have festivals, and say, 'of course we must all work for a festival . . .' They feel that they should pray, so they say, 'Of course we must all pray now . . .' They come up to me and say, 'You must give us a lecture . . .' "

I said: "Then why don't you tell them just to wait until you do have some teachings for them; until you have the right people at the right place at the right time?"

"I have tried that," he said, "but they don't listen, or else they desert me."

"But how do you square it with your conscience when you find that you are agreeing with all their demands?"

"We have come to an arrangement. I have got them to agree always to say, 'We do have to have a religious service, don't we?', whenever they want to do something. And I always answer 'Yes' loudly, and 'but not yet' under my breath."

To me this comes under the 'humour of the situation', even if not intended as a joke . . .

People often ask Sufis what is wrong with being cultivated, and why sensitivity should not accompany proper behaviour. The experienced fact is that of priorities. If a house is on fire, you will act accordingly, and your etiquette will be thrown to the winds. This does not mean that you are a boor, or want to be one.

We should note, too, that time is lost on ceremonial if something more effective could have been done instead.

Action

Nasrudin was sitting at a cafe table gazing at two men by a hole in the road.

"What are you thinking, Mulla?" asked a passer-by.

"How lazy people are. I have been sitting here for four hours, and I've never taken my eyes off those men. Can you believe that during all that time, neither of them has done any work?"

There are many jokes about the difference between how the Sufi sees something — the Reality — and the pre-occupations of most other people surrounding him — the ritual. The Sufi is often the victim of this charade called everyday life. Indeed, he needs a great deal of skill in planning to avoid discomfort and more. The greatest Sufis have been (most of these still are) venerated and turned almost into objects of worship: one example of misunderstanding, of people craving idolatry, not knowledge. Many have been murdered, even by court execution orders, for apostasy. More still have been called idiots, since this is the only conclusion that the ordinary person can reach about the behaviour which is linked with 'something beyond'. How could such a phenomenon not produce a mass of jokes?

Intention

There was once a Sufi who found himself in a large mass of people milling about outside the palace of the king of his country. The King had ordered that all the famous people of his realm were to be assembled and odes recited in their honour; the court poets had been working for months to get their verses ready, and this was the day of the great Gathering of Honour.

The Royal Guards separated the guests from the onlookers but the Sufi began to say: "I don't want to be praised, I don't want to be honoured, I don't want an ode in homage to me to be recited . . ." This, however, was to no avail, for the guards hustled him into the audience-chamber. He was struggling so hard (others only resisted from locally conventional modesty) that the King ordered him to be seated next to the Throne. Then the King ordered the King of Poets to recite the ode in honour of this most modest of men. The poem was nowhere to be found. They asked the sage his name, but nobody could remember who he was, if anyone. Finally the King asked him to say something. He said: "I do not want to be praised!"

"Why not?" demanded the King; "If you didn't want to be praised you should not have come to the reception!"

"But I didn't come — your guards picked me up in the street. I wasn't invited . . . All I was doing was saying that I DID NOT WANT TO BE PRAISED . . ."

The Sufi is an idiot to the outward man, the other is an oaf to the Sufi. The second seldom persists in dealing with the Sufi, luckily, which gives the latter a greater chance of teaching those who can learn than he would otherwise have. The Sufi will persist, coming back to the point again and again, because he knows that his jokes and other techniques are generally laying down a basis of understanding which will eventually amount to a sound seed bed. The following tale is employed both to illustrate the doctrine of 'time, place and people' and also to encourage the hearer, who may be able to conceive that his understanding may be weak but that it may also develop. He is, of course, the 'first disciple' of the tale. The fact that the Sufi has, in the story, accepted him at all, is the point of hope that his obtuseness will eventually yield to something worthwhile:

Deduction

A certain sage had two disciples; the first one was very argumentative and the second silent. Day after day, week in, week out, for year upon year, the first disciple answered the wise man back, refused to obey his orders, misunderstood what was said to him, badgered him for 'teachings' and explanations, and generally made life most uncomfortable.

Finally, after a number of years, the old teacher walked into a room where the disciples were sitting with a friend, pointed his finger at the silent disciple — and the man was instantly illuminated.

"Now, look at that", said the visitor. "If you had heeded the sage like the Silent One did, things might have been different!"

"Not on your life!" answered the awkward customer, "The Sage may have gone into action at last — but who softened him up?"

How to tell

People are always saying things like "How can I become a Sufi without a teacher? After all, lots of famous ones did . . ."

You have to give them a memorable illustration which will fix the contention that circumstances alter cases. A joke like the following one will help, not because it is strictly relevant in the sense of being a parable or parallel, but because the amusement engendered helps to operate on a similar level to the other person's expectation:

Ducks

A traveller went up to a peasant and asked whether he could wade through a certain stream. The man assured him that he could. When he was less than half way across, however, the man found his head almost under water, and he had to trudge back to the bank, where the countryman was still sitting.

"I thought you said that the water wasn't too deep for

me to cross, you fool . . ." he shouted.

"Can't make it out, you know" said the yokel, "it never comes more than halfway up the ducks . . ."

But if the student can learn to see himself as essentially a yokel in the land of the Sufis, how can he also know whether he is in that land or not? Which teacher is a true one, which is a fraud or himself self-deluded?

Sufis themselves have always provided innumerable stories for intending students. Most of them are based on the principle that the student must study the master to see by his words and actions whether he is working on a higher level, or whether he is merely a social phenomenon. The objection to this — that the student cannot tell, since the master is working in an invisible realm — is true only up to a point. When a supposed Sufi teacher manifests ordinary foibles or weaknesses as a part of his life's pattern, and if the student has also done enough interior work to give him an accurate judging capacity, the truth will be evident. This is why Sufis provide material, concurrently, on how to set aside prejudices and also on what unworthy teachers are like in their behaviour. This is a good example:

Gold for Everyone

There was a certain mystical master teacher — or, at any rate, someone who thought he was one. The only difficulty was that he had no disciples. He harangued and behaved mysteriously, but nothing happened.

One day he was complaining to a sort of wandering monk that he would give a silver piece for every disciple that the other one could bring in. "No problem at all" said the monk, "I have a lot of experience in these things. Let me have until tomorrow morning."

Soon after dawn the mystic awoke with the sound of thousands of people shouting his name as they collected on the town square. As he hurried out of his house to approach his eager audience, the monk stepped forward. "How was that?" "Marvellous, but I have to go and talk to them, or they'll come here and drag me out to address them." "You owe me 3,000 silver pieces" said the monk, and would not let him go until he had them.

As the monk was going off, the mystic said: "Well, I'm made now, thank you, thank you. But what did you tell them about me to get that degree of enthusiasm for mystical secrets at this time in the morning?"

"It was quite easy really. I told them all how wonderful you were — and that you would give out bags of gold in the town square at dawn!"

It should also be remembered, especially by those who want a tidy world, with the sacred and profane neatly labelled and visible in neat institutions, that false teachers unwittingly provide an excellent social service for the true ones. Like attracts like, and those who want sensationalism or stage orientals can have their fill and leave the serious workers alone as having insufficient attraction-value.

I am fond of this statement about the situation:

Too late

An angel winged her way from celestial realms to attend to a certain matter on Earth.

As she was about to alight on the planet, she met another angel homeward bound, to report.

"What are you doing here?" asked the second angel.

"I am going to illuminate a certain mystic, who will now at last be promoted to high rank!"

"You are too late", said the returning angel, "He has already been made head of his own Order of monks."

It has not escaped the attention of some sociologists, if not many metaphysicians, that whole countries which have the reputation of being filled with spiritual people are only occupied by people who imagine that they are engaged in spiritual pursuits. There is an ancient tale which shows how widespread this has always been, even in the East, 'home of spirituality':

Visitors

There was once a king who decided to treat everyone in prison more humanely. He ordained, among other things, that all convicts must have visitors, and his officers took the names of the towns and villages from which these people came, to make announcements that they must visit such-and-such people to cheer them up and prepare them for eventual release.

But there was one man who still never got any visitors. Finally the prison governor called him.

"You said that you have relatives and friends from such-and-such a village."

"Yes."

"We have sent criers around the countryside proclaiming that it is the King's command that you be visited. Why will your own people not present themselves here for this humanitarian purpose and to fulfil the requirements of this Royal Decree?"

"Probably because they are all convicts here already!"

There is very little that people can do for themselves when they belong to a community (sometimes it is a whole culture) which imagines that its social behaviour is spiritual. Such people manage to escape when they can see the hypocrisy of outward show and the perceptive shallowness of the emotional (which they always call 'deep'). From time to time, of course, this happens, and people sometimes wander from one 'mystical master' to another, until they discover what higher knowledge really is, by elimination:

The Limp

A man was limping as he walked down a street, and wincing with pain.

A doctor stopped him and said: "If I were you, I'd get yourself seen to; you need your appendix out."

So he had his appendix out. Presently he went to another doctor, claiming that he still had the same trouble. So he was put on a course of tranquillisers. This didn't help, and he went to a hospital, where they prescribed him a diet and remedial exercises.

Some weeks later he was strolling in the park and met one of his many doctors. "Glad to see you are better" said the physician, "and that I could be of service."

"'Service my eye" said the patient, "both the pain and the limp went away the moment I took that nail out of my shoe!"

Scoffers may see this as a tale which exposes the absurdity of all forms of higher knowledge being veridical. We note, however, that it signals the emerging capacity to 'walk'.

What was the 'nail' that the man took out of his shoe? The self-importance which the 'doctors' had encouraged: it is a deeply rooted (and for short-term purposes useful) instrument, but usually not a servant but a master:

People will swear to it

"What is your occupation?" the Judge asked Mulla Nasrudin when he was a witness in a court case.

"I am the greatest man in the world" said the Mulla.

After the case one of his friends said: "Nasrudin, why did you say that?"

"Yes", said the Mulla, "it is rather a pity — but I had to tell them just this once: I was on oath, you see."

Among the jokes which are employed to display the structure of a situation is the one about the boatman and the traveller.

Hold On . . .

A traveller was crossing a very broad stretch of water when the boat began to rock, so he caught hold of the mast with both hands to prevent himself being swept overboard.

While all this was happening the boatman, who of course was used to this kind of motion, made his way hand over hand along a rope and asked him for his fare.

"Certainly", said the traveller, "you just hold onto the mast like I am to keep me steady, and I'll get it out of my bag!"

The choice of interpretation of the tale tells us something about the person to whom we tell it. Some people think it means that teachers don't give adequate thought to their disciples: they expect them to do something which they cannot, though these things are easy to the teacher — who is, of course, the boatman in this case. Others say that this story shows that all disciples are foolish, since they imagine that someone can do something for them that they have to do for themselves. We regard this story as showing that there are many so-called mystical masters who are asking the disciple to do things which will, if they try to do them, sweep them away from real understanding, just as the storm would sweep away this passenger when faced by the idiotic demand of the boatman. "He may be a boatman, but he does not necessarily know the real pattern of events — sea-legs do not go with intelligence."

Obsession

Jokes are used as correctives to help people who adopt, for instance, single-minded attitudes which prevent their further understanding. Sufi study is graded so that once an objective is reached, it has to be forgotten, while concentration is directed to the next objective.

One neat reminder of this one is about the prayer-beads: Someone studying to be a Sufi once read that "if you make all your concerns one concern, you will achieve your desire." This man wanted, more than anything else, to be reincarnated. He spent many years telling beads and concentrating upon reincarnation.

They do say — though I cannot vouch for it — that he did come back after he died — as a rosary . . .

What happens to people who do not learn from Sufi jokes? Those, for example, who think that they appreciate them, but only do so because others have insisted that these tales are important or have 'inner significances'?

We must follow a Sufi observer on a long trip, while he sees what happens to the literalists:

A Precedent

A famous and greatly-respected fakir presented himself at the gates of Heaven, to find them closed, with only a single angel on guard. When he was asked his name, the fakir felt that deeds were better than words.

He went through his whole repertoire. First he made things appear and disappear, then he blew fire from his mouth. Next he materialized a whole assembly of eighty thousand disciples from his earthly life. Finally he aimed a burst of special power at the angel: the type reserved for really convincing people on Earth of his holy marvellousness.

"All right," said the angel, "I'll open the door: but I don't think, somehow, that you're going to like it in there . . ."

On another occasion, we are told, someone who specialised in organising Sufi knowledge into an academic form also died:

Honour where honour is due

A whole band of Sufis were being admitted to Heaven, and the doors swung open just enough to let each one in. As soon as he was in, without any ceremony, the doors closed and then opened for the next, who went in without any hesitation, as if he was quite expecting to be admitted.

Right at the end came a scholar, with a reverend beard and majestic gait, large turban and confident look. As he stepped forward the gates swung open, and trumpets sounded, while tremendous applause broke out from an assembled multitude.

A shining figure came forward to escort him within.

"This is most gratifying," said the scholar to himself, "to know that the learned no longer will have to give themselves airs and graces. Here, at least, our importance is recognized." To the apparition he said: "Why all this ceremony?"

"Well," said the angel, "it is something of an occasion. You see, this is the first time that we have had an academic among us . . ."

The Reality

It is quite possible that the academic 'Sufi' was also the one about whom the next story is told. Its mystical master seems to have less awareness of what is really going on than the man who came to learn from him.

When you see the masses of polite and stereotyped people interested in spiritual studies here in the West, and the readiness with which they are accepted by their spiritual masters, it is a great contrast to the way things are with many schools in the East. There it is generally considered an honour and a rarity to be admitted as a disciple. In fact there is a well-known story about it, which may have less currency here . . .

The difficulty

There is one teacher who only accepts a single student every three years, and it is related that when he indicated that he was willing to interview applicants, there was only one applicant.

"Very good" he said, "I will accept you on probation. But you should not overdo the austerities. I do not require my pupils to be so covered in mud and ashes, with clothes torn to ribbons and lacerated faces . . ."

"Then," said the successful applicant, "you wouldn't have wanted any of the three hundred other applicants I had to fight to stay in the running — they were all in a very shocking condition . . ."

A man who had once been an obtuse disciple of the type so often complained about, and who later became a Sufi, told me how he had escaped from circular thinking by seeing the structure of this joke:

Cause and effect

A man sent an advertisement to his local newspaper offering a reward of a thousand gold pieces for the finder of his pet bird, which had escaped. When publication day arrived, the paper did not come out. He telephoned the office to find out why, and was answered by the cleaning woman. "I am sorry, there's nobody here to talk to you," she said, "because everyone is out looking for your bird."

This tale can also be used to illustrate the kind of situation which arises when everyone tries to pursue his or her personal interest in the quest for higher knowledge, forgetting that there is an essential need to maintain the community through which this awareness is in fact communicated.

In case this last emphasis sets too many people off forming their own metaphysical groups and — as will always happen without proper understanding — simply forming circuses, it should be restated that random groups are not Sufi ones at all . . .

The caution which I have just shown in not provoking reckless and ill-informed activity might be reflected in another story. This putatively concerns a discussion between a dervish writing a book for circulation in the West, who showed the manuscript to a certain knowledgeable Sufi.

Export model

Dervish: "What did you think of the book written for the people of the West?"

Sufi: "Perfectly balanced".

Dervish: "In what way?"

Sufi: "If it had been on any higher level, they wouldn't have understood it. But if it had been any lower, anyone would have been ashamed of it . . ."

I know what he meant; but so too do quite a lot of people both in the East and West, for no culture has a monopoly of almost hopeless learners. Still, one needs fortitude to continue in this area in the West, since Sufis are still often viewed as oddities and not, as in the East, recognisable as established mentors when they are genuine. This Western joke shows that people in their culture, too, find it unprofitable to try to inform others who really should get rid of hangups first:

Please Yourself

"Could you tell me the time?"

"Certainly. It is three o'clock."

"But it can't be later than half-past two!"

"All right, then — please yourself!"

I have heard a Jewish joke, too, which was once tacked onto this one:

Consequences

Someone asked the man with the watch why he did not insist that the time was really what he knew it was.

"If I had told him the right time, he would have talked some more. Then I'd have taken him home, and he might have wanted to marry my daughter. How could I marry my daughter to a man who sits in cafes at three in the afternoon? So I told him something which would stop him talking!"

The Sufi might say that the man with the watch in the first joke was simply trying to stress the other man's looseness of thinking: the tendency in everyone to dispute something because it is not comfortable to accept it. In the second joke he would find an intimation that although people may act irrationally, there is usually a deep rationality — or rationale — in what they say or do. This is the operation of the 'Commanding Self' which Sufi teaching and activity is designed to identify and outwit.

In jokes, as much as in anything, we see the differences between the Sufi procedures and those of other persuasions powerfully illustrated. Someone once tried to make a humorous statement about this:

The Difference
It has been said that the difference between the Sufi and the ordinary man is that the one is aware of what is really important and the other usually unaware — even of trifles — which are useful at the time. The Sufi, they say, pursuing the thesis by the shock method may be a man who, joining the army, might save the lives of everyone in the regiment by shooting the cook: Sufism is very much exclusion as well as inclusion. But, in the same military situation, the disciple is one who stays up until three in the morning wondering what he has forgotten: until he remembers that it was that he had to go to bed early . . .

TEACHINGS OF RUMI
'THE MASNAVI'

Jalaluddin Rumi's great work, *The Masnavi*, was 43 years in the writing. During the past seven hundred years, this book, called by Iranians 'The Koran in Persian', a tribute paid to no other book, has occupied a central place in Sufism.

'*The Masnavi* is full of profound mysteries, and a most important book in the study of Sufism — mysteries which must, for the most part, be left to the discernment of the reader.'

F. Hadland Davis

'To the Sufi, if not to anyone else, this book speaks from a different dimension, yet a dimension which is in a way within his deepest self'.

Idries Shah

'The greatest mystical poet of any age'.

Professor R. A. Nicolson

'It can well be argued that he is the supreme mystical poet of all mankind'.

Professor A. J. Arberry

Teachings of Rumi 'The Masnavi',
Abridged & translated by E. H. Whinfield.
The Octagon Press (Hardback & Paperback).

THE SPIRIT OF THE EAST

Today the kinship of all religious thought and dogma is becoming more apparent to mankind — and the value of Oriental thought to the Occidental mind is obvious. Here is a selection from Moslem, Parsee, Hindu, Hebrew, Confucian and other sources, chosen not only for their spiritual worth but also for the particular virtues of each creed which they represent.

The aim of this book is to introduce readers to the religious thought of the East, which — for reasons of language and other difficulties — they might otherwise have considered inaccessible.

The Spirit of the East,
by Sirdar Ikbal Ali Shah.
The Octagon Press (Hardback).

FOLK TALES OF CENTRAL ASIA

A collection of stories selected entirely from the oral tradition: from servants and royal courts, from teahouses and caravanserais — some of them just ahead of the industrial development which helped to wipe out such delightful examples of the treasures of human culture.

Amina Shah, who was brought up both in the East and West, has written and broadcast extensively on Eastern traditional lore.

Folk Tales of Central Asia,
by Amina Shah.
The Octagon Press (Hardback).

THE DERMIS PROBE

The title-story, with script by Idries Shah, filmed as a space-satire, was chosen as an Outstanding Film of the Year and selected for showing at both the London and New York film festivals. This is a collection of extracts from the written and oral tradition of Eastern thinkers.

Shah says in his Preface:

'In this book you can find illustrated some of the peculiarities of thought in the Country which is today's world, seen by its inhabitants and by those who call themselves visitors.'

". . . a peep-show into a world which most people do not know exists".
— *The Guardian*

". . . deftly done, in the true Sufi tradition".
— *The Times Literary Supplement*

". . . whisking away the rug from under our favourite convictions and thinking habits . . . the effect is exhilarating".
— *Tribune*

The Dermis Probe,
by Idries Shah.
Jonathan Cape Ltd., (Hardback).

THE SECRET GARDEN OF MAHMUD SHABISTARI

This book, by an almost unknown Persian sage of the thirteenth century, is among the greatest classics of spirituality of the East.

Though written over six hundred years ago, as a reviewer correctly pointed out, 'Shabistari's ideas can usefully be applied to our own contemporary social problems.'

John A. Subhan says of it:

'His work is important out of all comparison . . . because it is a compendium of Sufi terminology in the form of question and answer.'

The Secret Garden of Mahmud Shabistari, translated by Johnson Pasha.
The Octagon Press (Hardback).

THE PLEASANTRIES OF THE INCREDIBLE MULLA NASRUDIN

Incomparably illustrated by Richard Williams and Errol le Cain.

Both this book — containing no less than 165 tales — and the previous Nasrudin volume have been acclaimed for their humour by critics all over the world. Nasrudin tales have been used to illustrate abstruse concepts in high-energy physics: and a complete system of mystical training based upon them was described in the *Hibbert Journal*.

'Parallel to the mind's workings'   — *The Observer*

'A rare gift — healing laughter'   — *New Society*

'Undebased wisdom — an extension of the proverbial'
                                          — *Country Life*

The Pleasantries of the Incredible Mulla Nasrudin, by Idries Shah.
Jonathan Cape Ltd., (Hardback).

THE EXPLOITS OF THE INCOMPARABLE MULLA NASRUDIN

The first collection of Nasrudin stories acclaimed as a humourous masterpiece, as a collection of the finest jokes, as a priceless gift book, and for its hundred 'enchanted tales'.

But this folklore figure's antics have also been divined as 'mirroring the antics of the mind'. They have a double use: when the jokes have been enjoyed, their psychological significance starts to sink in. Idries Shah has achieved a true breakthrough with a book which can convulse on the level of humour and still get serious reviews, like this one from the sociological journal *New Society:*

'His stories are perfectly designed, harmless models for isolating and holding for a moment the distortions of the mind which so often pass for reasonable behaviour'.

'Arouse laughter in the simple and contemplation in the illuminated'   — *The Listener*

'Sharp English that doesn't waste a word'
                                   — *Sunday Telegraph*

'Humorous Masterpiece'   — *Birmingham Post*

'Our familiar responses are ruled out'
                                   — *New Statesman*

'All will welcome the telling by Idries Shah'
                                   — *Times Educational Supplement*

**The Exploits of the Incomparable Mulla Nasrudin
by Idries Shah.
Jonathan Cape Ltd, (Hardback).**

WISDOM OF THE IDIOTS

Narratives of the action-philosophy of the thinkers who called themselves 'idiots' in contrast to the self-styled 'wise'. The first edition of this book was widely acclaimed for its entertainment value and psychological interest.

The celebrated writer Nina Epton said in a recent broadcast:

'Seeds that Idries Shah sows on our Western path are chosen by a discerning modern mind, with a profound knowledge of the East and West. The best spiritual traditions, interpreted afresh, are applied by Idries Shah to our contemporary world. This is his contribution to our spiritual equipment — which consequently now finds itself considerably enriched.'

'Opens up a new world of understanding'
— *The Inquirer*

'Rare examples of non-linear thinking'
— *Evening News*

Wisdom of the Idiots,
by Idries Shah.
The Octagon Press (Hardback).